W9-AVI-709

JAMES BUCHANAN
OUR FIFTEENTH PRESIDENT

by Gerry and Janet Souter

THE CHILD'S WORLD®

The Child's World

PUBLISHED IN THE UNITED STATES OF AMERICA

THE CHILD'S WORLD®
1980 Lookout Drive • Mankato, MN 56003-1705
800-599-READ • www.childsworld.com

ACKNOWLEDGMENTS
The Child's World®: Mary Berendes, Publishing Director

Creative Spark: Mary McGavic, Project Director; Melissa McDaniel, Editorial
Director; Deborah Goodsite, Photo Research

The Design Lab: Kathleen Petelinsek, Design; Gregory Lindholm, Page Production

Content Adviser: David R. Smith, Adjunct Assistant Professor of History,
University of Michigan–Ann Arbor

PHOTOS
Cover and page 3: White House Historical Association (White House Collection),
(detail)

Interior: Alamy: 14 (Visual Arts Library (London)); The Art Archive: 19 (National
History Museum Mexico City/Gianni Dagli Ort), 32 (Culver Pictures); Art
Resource: 18, 23 and 38 (National Portrait Gallery, Smithsonian Institution);
Corbis: 21, 36 and 39 (Corbis), 26, 28 (Bettmann); Dickinson College, Carlisle,
PA: 6 (Archives and Special Collections); Getty Images: 4 (POPPERFOTO), 5
and 38, 27 (Getty Images); The Granger Collection, New York: 8, 15, 17, 20,
22, 25, 31, 34, 35, 37; The Hermitage, Home of Andrew Jackson, Nashville,
Tennessee: 12; The Image Works: 13 and 39 (Topham), 29 (Mary Evans Picture
Library); iStockphoto: 44 (Tim Fan); Courtesy of Lancaster County Historical
Society, Lancaster, Pennsylvania: 10; Library of Congress: 16; Picture History: 30;
SuperStock, Inc.: 9 (SuperStock); U.S. Air Force photo: 45.

LIBRARY OF CONGRESS CATALOGING-IN-PUBLICATION DATA
Souter, Gerry.
  James Buchanan / by Gerry and Janet Souter.
      p. cm. — (Presidents of the U.S.A.)
  Includes bibliographical references and index.
  ISBN 978–1–60253–044–7 (library bound : alk. paper)
  1. Buchanan, James, 1791–1868—Juvenile literature. 2. Presidents—United
States—Biography—Juvenile literature. I. Souter, Janet, 1940– II. Title. III. Series.

E437.S678 2008
973.6'8092—dc22
[B]
                                        2008002297

James Buchanan
served as president
from 1857 to 1861.

TABLE OF CONTENTS

FROM SCHOOLBOY TO POLITICIAN

James Buchanan, was born on April 23, 1791, in Cove Gap, Pennsylvania. He was the first son of Elizabeth Speer Buchanan and James Buchanan. His sister Mary was born two years earlier. Although Mary died shortly after James was born, the family grew over the years. By the time James reached adulthood, he had four sisters and four brothers. In 1796, the family moved to the small town of Mercersburg, Pennsylvania. James loved the surrounding countryside and the simple life of a quiet village. It was a love that stayed with him throughout his life.

James's father was a successful merchant. He also kept a small farm. In Mercersburg, Mr. Buchanan purchased a two-story building that served as both the family home and his store. From his father, James learned about running a

James Buchanan in 1841

business and about the importance of keeping accurate records. His mother taught him to enjoy poetry. Together, she and James read the works of popular poets of the time.

At age 16, James was already prepared for college. He enrolled at Dickinson College in the nearby town of Carlisle. Although he received good grades in college, James often found himself in trouble with his teachers. They thought he spent too much time having fun with his friends. Near the end of his time at Dickinson, his teachers threatened to make him leave school because of his behavior.

James Buchanan was born in this log cabin in Cove Gap, Pennsylvania. As his father became more successful, the family moved to a larger home in Mercersburg, Pennsylvania.

Dr. John King, a pastor and a Buchanan family friend, spoke to the school. Fortunately, the school agreed to let James finish his final year. During that time, he stayed out of trouble and did well in class.

When it came time for James to graduate, he was chosen to receive senior honors. Only two students could receive the award. But the teachers refused to give him the honors, because they remembered him as a troublemaker. This made James angry. James's father said it was better to accept the decision. Doing that would make him more of a man. The school finally decided to let James make a graduation speech but did not award him the senior honor. In later years, this experience taught James how to deal with disappointments.

Buchanan attended Dickinson College in the small town of Carlisle. Dickinson was established in 1783, making it one of the nation's oldest colleges.

After leaving Dickinson, Buchanan decided to study law. Because he was the oldest son, his father wanted him to have a good income in case he ever needed to help support the family. Buchanan was eager to succeed, so he worked and studied hard all day. In the evenings after he finished work, he practiced making speeches. He understood that a lawyer must be comfortable speaking in front of people. Buchanan passed his law exams in 1813, and he was ready to open his own law office. Within a short time, he had a busy and successful career in Lancaster, Pennsylvania.

As a lawyer, Buchanan traveled all over southern Pennsylvania and handled many different types of cases. He wrote wills, took care of property claims, and drew up contracts. He became well-known among the region's politicians. He joined several political organizations and became president of the Washington Association. This group supported the **Federalists,** one of the major **political parties** of the day. The Federalists were in favor of having a central bank of the United States. A central bank would issue paper money, which would help make the U.S. economy more stable. Buchanan thought this would help the United States as it fought the War of 1812 against Great Britain. But President James Madison refused to consider a central bank. Buchanan spoke out against Madison and the way he handled the war.

In 1814, Buchanan decided to run for the state legislature. A legislature is the part of a government that makes laws. But in August, he heard that the

In Buchanan's day, there were only three law schools in the United States. Young men who wanted to be lawyers simply had to take an oral test in their state. After passing this test, called the bar examination, they usually went to work for experienced lawyers to learn the business. They would later set up their own practice.

British troops marched through Washington, D.C., on August 24, 1814, setting fire to government buildings. They burned the White House and buildings housing the Library of Congress, the Senate, and the House of Representatives.

When British forces threatened Baltimore, Buchanan joined a group of **volunteers** who were eager for adventure. They were ordered to travel to a town four miles outside of Baltimore and steal or borrow horses for American soldiers. After the volunteers acquired the horses, their services were no longer needed, and Buchanan returned to Lancaster.

British had attacked Washington, D.C. They had set the White House, the Capitol, and other government buildings on fire. Then the British marched toward the city of Baltimore, Maryland. Buchanan decided to join the army. A few weeks after he joined, the Americans began to win the war. In late December, the two nations signed a peace treaty, an agreement to end the war.

By then, Buchanan had been elected to the Pennsylvania House of Representatives. He was about to start on a career in **politics.**

CHAPTER TWO

THE ROAD TO THE SENATE

Buchanan was reelected to the Pennsylvania House in 1815. He was on the road to an impressive career in politics. There were several reasons for his success. Buchanan spoke clearly, and he looked at problems from different viewpoints. People called him a "hair splitter" because he was so concerned with details.

James Buchanan was just 24 years old when he entered the Pennsylvania House of Representatives.

9

This photo from 1866 shows the busy street in Lancaster, Pennsylvania, where Buchanan had his law office. His office was in the building at the center of the photo.

By this time, Buchanan believed that there should not be a single, large bank that controlled all of the government's money. He believed it was wrong to let a small group of people have so much power. The question of a central bank would not be settled for more than a decade, when Andrew Jackson was the president.

In 1816, Buchanan decided to leave politics and return to his law practice in Lancaster. Two years later, he met Ann Coleman, a young woman from a wealthy Lancaster family. He asked her to marry him in 1819, and Ann accepted. But she and her family canceled the wedding plans in November of that year. She had heard rumors that James was seeing another woman, and that he was only marrying her for her family's money. Then, while on a visit to Philadelphia, Ann became ill and died.

Buchanan was heartbroken. He sent letters to her father, asking to see Ann's body before she was buried. "I feel that happiness has fled from me forever," he wrote. Mr. Coleman returned the letters unopened.

Buchanan was so sad that he left Lancaster and his law practice. He was gone for several weeks. He did not want to be in a town filled with unhappy memories. Finally, a friend suggested that he run for the U.S. Congress. Perhaps that would help to take his mind off Ann's death. In 1820, Buchanan was elected to the U.S. House of Representatives. He moved to Washington, D.C., to start a new life.

Buchanan served in the House of Representatives for 10 years. During that time, tensions grew between the northern and southern states. The year before Buchanan was elected, Missouri settlers asked the government to make their **territory** a state. But would Missouri allow slavery? Northerners did not want slavery to spread into new parts of the country. Southerners did not want the nation to have more **free states** than slave states. Many were afraid that if slavery did not expand with the country, it would eventually be outlawed in the South as well. Most southerners thought that states should have more power than the **federal** government. They believed the **Constitution** did not give the federal government the right to tell states whether they could allow slavery.

In 1820, the people of Maine also asked to become a state. Finally, Congress made a **compromise.** It decided that Maine would be admitted to the **Union**

James Buchanan is the only president who never married.

In 1820, James Monroe ran again for president as a member of the Democratic-Republican Party. He won 231 out of 232 **electoral votes**. The Federalists had faded away, and there seemed to be only one political party in the country. Because there was little anger between members of opposing political parties, this time was known as "the Era of Good Feeling."

In 1831, a teacher named Prudence Crandall of Maryland was sent to prison for admitting black girls to her school.

as a free state. Missouri would be a slave state. This way, the number of free and slave states would remain equal. There would be 12 of each. In addition, Congress divided the continent in half at a **latitude** of 36 degrees, 30 minutes. From that time forward, slavery would be legal in all areas south of that latitude. In all areas north of it, slavery would be illegal. This decision became known as the Missouri Compromise. For many years, the Missouri Compromise seemed to work. But it could not keep both sides happy forever.

By 1828, the Democratic-Republicans were called simply the Democrats. That year, Democrat Andrew Jackson was elected president, and Buchanan was

Andrew Jackson was elected president in 1828. He and Buchanan shared many ideas about how the U.S. government should work.

12

Washington, D.C., looked very different in Buchanan's day. There was lots of open space and some areas were still being used as farmland. The picture of the Capitol above is from around 1850.

reelected to the House of Representatives. Buchanan wanted to support Jackson in any way he could. In 1831, President Jackson offered Buchanan the post of **minister** to Russia. In this position, Buchanan would be in charge of U.S. relations with Russia.

Buchanan was unsure whether to accept the president's offer. For one thing, he didn't speak French. At the time, French was the language spoken by **diplomats.** But Buchanan finally accepted the job and began taking French lessons. In March 1832, he left for St. Petersburg, the capital of Russia.

Buchanan arrived in Russia in late spring. He found life there to be very different from that in the United States. The chilly June weather forced him to wear a warm cloak, even in the daytime. Yet at that time of year, the sky was so bright and the days so

Buchanan was unhappy in St. Petersburg. He found it to be too cold and too far away from home.

long that he could read without a candle until midnight. Buchanan found the country strange. He wrote to President Jackson that "there is no freedom of the press, no public opinion, and but little political conversation." The Russian people worried that they would be punished if they spoke out against their government. As an American who was guaranteed freedom of speech by the Constitution, this was difficult for Buchanan to understand.

While in St. Petersburg, Buchanan made an agreement that allowed the United States to use Russia's Black Sea as a trade route. It took several months before Russian leaders agreed to sign the treaty, but Buchanan finally convinced them. About the same time, Great

Britain also wanted to make such an agreement with Russia. But their minister could not reach an agreement with the Russian government.

By 1833, Buchanan wanted to return to the United States. He found the cold Russian winters difficult, and he longed to see his family again. Buchanan's mother had died in the spring of that year, but he had not received the news until July. He felt he was too far from home. He had also heard that Pennsylvania's citizens wanted him to run for the Senate. In August, he began the long journey back to Pennsylvania.

The next year, Buchanan was elected to the U.S. Senate. The two main issues at the time were banking and slavery. Buchanan argued fiercely against a new law that Senator Henry Clay had suggested. It would allow people who owed large amounts of money to declare bankruptcy. This meant that people could be

Later in life, Buchanan was nicknamed "Old Buck."

Henry Clay gives a speech in the Senate. Clay was a leading senator who often opposed Jackson and the Democrats.

At the time Buchanan was a senator, Washington, D.C., was more like a small farm town than a grand capital. Chickens, geese, and pigs wandered the unpaved streets. Canals and waterways gave off a foul odor. It's no wonder that Buchanan escaped to his Pennsylvania estate whenever he could.

freed from their **debts** by going to court and asking for the government's help. Buchanan was against the idea. He thought it would create too much work for the nation's courts and cost the government too much money. He also believed that bankruptcy would make it too easy for people to borrow money without ever paying it back. He felt sorry for people with money problems, but he was more concerned with upholding the law.

The problem of slavery was becoming ever more troublesome. Although Buchanan did not like slavery, he believed that slaveholders had certain rights. Southern states had been admitted to the Union years before as slave states. How could the government take away that right so many years later? In addition, the

The labor of enslaved workers made many southern landowners wealthy. By 1860, the United States was home to four million enslaved people.

U.S. Constitution protects people's belongings, and enslaved people were considered property, just like a house or livestock. Buchanan thought that taking away property from the nation's citizens was a dangerous thing for a government to do—even if that "property" was a human being. He believed that the states should have the right to decide whether to allow slavery.

Buchanan saw no way to forbid slavery in the southern states without damaging the Union. Even though he did not like the fact that one human being could own another, he did not join forces with the **abolitionists** who wanted to end slavery. His main concern was keeping the Union together.

Buchanan was also a firm believer in the nation's westward expansion. Most congressmen and presidents during that time felt the same way. Buchanan spoke strongly about it. In 1837, he said, "Prevent the

In the 1830s, many Americans believed that the United States was destined to expand across the continent. This painting, called The Course of Empire, *shows Americans moving steadily west to build new towns.*

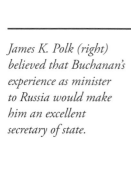

Between 1790 and 1860, 21 states were admitted to the Union.

American People from crossing the Rocky Mountains? You might as well command [the] Niagara [Falls] not to flow. We must fulfill our destiny." The belief that the United States should spread all the way to the Pacific Ocean would come to be called "manifest destiny."

In the election of 1844, Democrats in Pennsylvania wanted Buchanan to run for president. But Buchanan knew he did not have enough support from people in other states. Instead, a southerner named James K. Polk received the **nomination.**

Buchanan planned to remain in the Senate. But when Polk became president, he chose Buchanan as his secretary of state. This put Buchanan in charge of the nation's relations with other countries. Although Buchanan had been reelected to the Senate, he accepted President Polk's offer and gave up his seat.

James K. Polk (right) believed that Buchanan's experience as minister to Russia would make him an excellent secretary of state.

THE MEXICO PROBLEM

Buchanan served as secretary of state under President James Polk. One of the most pressing issues at the time was whether Texas, then an independent nation, would become part of the United States. Mexico had once controlled Texas and did not want it to join the United States.

In 1845, Britain and France advised the Texas government not to join the Union. They did not want the United States to become more powerful in North America than it already was. If Texas were an independent nation, it might help keep the United States from expanding even farther across the continent.

The people of Texas were against the treaty. In fact, most of them wanted to join the Union. And Texas did join the United States in December 1845.

Then a new dispute arose over the location of the border between Mexico and Texas. Mexicans gathered along Texas's southern border. On April 25, 1846, the first shots were fired in the Mexican-American War. For the next two years, Generals Zachary Taylor and Winfield Scott fought their way across Mexico. When they captured Mexico City, the capital, the Mexicans were forced to give up. President Polk wanted to take over the whole country, but Buchanan convinced him to accept another option. In the end, a treaty gave the United States a huge piece of land. The treaty increased the nation's size by nearly 1.2 million square miles. The territory the United States gained makes up the states of Arizona, Nevada, California, and Utah, as well as parts of New Mexico, Colorado, and Wyoming.

APPROACHING STORM

I n 1848, Buchanan considered running for president, but the Democratic Party chose Lewis Cass instead. General Zachary Taylor, who had helped win the Mexican-American War that same year, won the election. Some Democrats thought Buchanan should run for the Senate, but he refused. He was 58 years old now and felt he needed a rest from Washington politics.

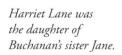

Buchanan bought Wheatland, a 22-acre estate near Lancaster, and returned to the Pennsylvania countryside. Still unmarried, he became the **mentor** to his nieces and nephews and their children. He helped many of his nephews find jobs in the government. To all, especially his favorite niece, Harriet Lane, he offered advice on how to behave. Both of Harriet's parents had died when she was 11, and she went to live with Buchanan. He sent her to one of the best girls' schools in the country. Harriet was

Harriet Lane was the daughter of Buchanan's sister Jane.

outgoing and friendly, but Buchanan wanted her to learn how to be a proper lady. When Harriet wasn't studying, she helped run Wheatland.

Buchanan did not lose touch with his political friends in Washington. Many still came to visit him at Wheatland, seeking his advice on government matters. By 1852, he was ready to return to politics—and to run for president.

The nation continued to be troubled by the issue of slavery. When the United States took over land in the West after the Mexican-American War, the country had to decide whether to allow slavery there. Congress

Buchanan bought Wheatland, a mansion in the Pennsylvania countryside, in 1848. It was his home until his death in 1868.

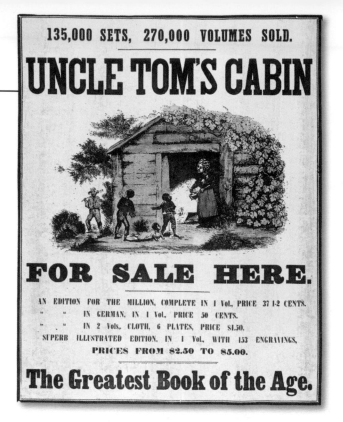

In 1852, Harriet Beecher Stowe wrote a book titled Uncle Tom's Cabin. *Stowe wanted the book to show the country how unjust and inhuman slavery was. People in the South thought Stowe was hateful. Northern readers were shocked to learn the horrors of the slavery system. The book sold more than 300,000 copies the first year. It was the best-selling novel of the 19th century.*

had tried to deal with the issue with the Compromise of 1850. It allowed California to enter the Union as a free state. The territories of New Mexico and Utah could decide for themselves whether to allow slavery. Buchanan believed this was wrong. He thought Congress should enforce the Missouri Compromise of 1820, which banned slavery in northern regions and allowed it in southern regions.

Buchanan didn't believe in slavery, yet he did not want the North to end slavery in the South. Because he was from a northern state but often favored the South, no one was sure where he stood on the issue. His main opponent for the 1852 Democratic presidential nomination was Stephen A. Douglas, a U.S. senator from Illinois. Douglas had been one of the leading supporters of the Compromise of 1850. He believed that the slavery question should be left to the people who live in each territory.

There was a deep division in the Democratic Party. Buchanan, Douglas, and the other leading **candidates** all faced strong hostility from various groups within the party. At the 1852 Democratic **convention,** none of them could gain the support of enough **delegates** to win the nomination. Buchanan said that he would not feel bad if he didn't get the nomination. He had been disappointed before, and he would retire if defeated. Finally, Democrats chose a compromise candidate, Franklin Pierce.

At the Democratic convention of 1852, delegates voted 34 times without being able to settle on a candidate. Finally, on their 35th try, they chose Franklin Pierce of New Hampshire. Many delegates had never heard of Pierce. All they knew about him was that he was a good speaker and that he had served in the Mexican-American War. And—perhaps more importantly—he had few enemies.

Buchanan wanted to run for president in 1848 and 1852, but the Democratic Party chose other candidates. He finally had his chance in 1856.

23

Queen Victoria
called Harriet Lane
"dear Miss Lane."

One problem Buchanan
had in Great Britain
was what to wear. The
American secretary
of state ordered
Buchanan to dress
simply, even on formal
occasions. Buchanan
obeyed and wore a
black coat, a white
vest, black pants,
and dress boots. He
added a sword, which
indicated that he was a
gentleman. The British
newspapers criticized
him for not wearing
gold, lace, and jewelry.
Americans supported
Buchanan, because
he was representing
his country's
democratic ideals.

Pierce went on to win the presidency. He offered Buchanan the post of minister to Great Britain. Harriet Lane joined him there in 1854. They had grown close over the years, and she was now a charming young lady. The British people admired her. Even Queen Victoria was delighted by Harriet's friendly personality.

Buchanan's service as minister to Great Britain was disappointing. He had hoped to encourage the British to stop setting up colonies in the Americas. But Great Britain was involved in a war against Russia, and its leaders were too busy to consider the issue.

Another problem was the matter of Cuba, an island about 90 miles off the southern tip of Florida. The United States wanted to buy Cuba from Spain, but Spain refused to sell it. President Pierce had Buchanan meet with the French and Spanish ministers in Ostend, Belgium, to try to force the sale. The result was a document known as the Ostend Manifesto, which said that if Spain wouldn't sell Cuba, the United States could take it by force. Parts of the Ostend Manifesto were published in American newspapers. This angered northerners. They feared that Cuba would become another slave state. Buchanan was blamed for the document, but a century later, historians found that President Pierce had added the "take it by force" remark.

By 1856, Buchanan was ready to return home. He left Britain in February and arrived home to find his country in turmoil. Tensions over slavery were at a boiling point. The problem was most severe in Kansas. In 1854, the Kansas-Nebraska Act had been passed.

It allowed the settlers of these territories to choose whether to accept or outlaw slavery. Pro- and antislavery forces battled in Kansas, leaving more than 200 people dead.

Buchanan believed he could find a way to end the serious problems his nation faced. He decided to run for president once more. This time, he won the Democratic nomination. Buchanan was personally against slavery and a northerner, so some people in the North voted for him. But he supported the right to own slaves, so many southerners voted for him as well. Buchanan ran against Republican John C. Frémont and won more than 58 percent of the vote.

Charles Sumner, a senator from Massachusetts, had sharply criticized the way Congress handled the situation in Kansas. During a speech in Congress, he insulted proslavery senators, including Andrew Butler of South Carolina. This made Butler's nephew, Representative Preston Brooks, angry. He beat Sumner unconscious with his walking stick.

It took Charles Sumner three years to recover from Preston Brooks's attack.

THE DRED SCOTT DECISION

Dred Scott was a slave owned by Dr. John Emerson of Missouri.
Emerson was a surgeon with the U.S. Army. In 1834, the army
sent Emerson to Illinois, where slavery was against the law. He
did not think he had to obey antislavery laws if the army sent
him to a free state, so he took Scott with him. Later, Scott and
Emerson moved to what is now Minnesota. Slavery was also
illegal there. Finally, in 1838, they returned to Missouri.

Scott believed that because he had lived in a free state and
a free territory, he should be considered a free man. In 1846,
he went to court in Missouri to sue for his freedom. He won
the case, but the Emerson family appealed the decision. This
meant they asked a more powerful court to consider the case.
Eventually, in 1857, the case reached the U.S. Supreme Court.

Most of the nine Supreme Court justices were from the South. Roger Taney (above), the chief justice of the Supreme Court, wrote the decision. The justices decided that traveling through free areas did not make a slave free. They argued that the Constitution made it illegal to take property away from any citizen. Since slaves were property, they could not be taken from their owners, regardless of whether they crossed into free territory. The justices also stated that people of African descent could not be citizens of the United States. Since Scott was not a citizen, he had no right to sue. The justices also ruled that Congress did not have the power to ban slavery in territories.

Scott was disappointed by the decision. But soon after, he was sold to Peter Blow, the son of his first owner. Blow freed him immediately. After a long battle for liberty, Scott was finally a free man.

MOVING TOWARD WAR

On March 4, 1857, James Buchanan and Vice President John Breckinridge arrived to take the oath of office at the Capitol. Most Americans believed that Buchanan was a good politician. They hoped he could solve the problems between the North and the South. At his **inauguration,** he said that there was a simple solution to the slavery issue.

James Buchanan was 65 years old when he became president.

Buchanan said that the U.S. Constitution protected slavery in the South, where it had always existed. If these states allowed slavery, how could the federal government outlaw it anywhere else in the country? Buchanan said that new territories should decide the issue for themselves.

Buchanan's argument was logical. But it did not recognize the fact that a growing number of Americans wanted to stop slavery from expanding into new territories. And some believed slavery was always wrong. They wanted it to be outlawed everywhere, even in the South where it had existed for hundreds of years.

At his inauguration, Buchanan said that the only way to solve the problem of slavery was "to leave the people of a territory free to decide their own destiny for themselves, subject only to the Constitution of the United States."

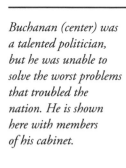

In 1860, the Prince of Wales, the man who would later become King Edward VII of Great Britain, visited Buchanan at the White House. So many guests came with the prince that Buchanan had to sleep in the hall.

Buchanan's stand on slavery would cause problems for him throughout his presidency. It would also lead the nation closer than ever to **civil war.**

Buchanan began his presidency by selecting a cabinet, the group of men who would advise him. He tried to choose people from both the North and the South. He wanted advisers who would strive to save the Union. Unfortunately, most of his cabinet did not want to end slavery.

In 1857, the country's economy was in serious trouble. Many companies went out of business. Banks closed. Farmers lost their land. In the North, workers rioted in the streets because they had neither jobs nor food. Buchanan did what he could to help

Buchanan (center) was a talented politician, but he was unable to solve the worst problems that troubled the nation. He is shown here with members of his cabinet.

rebuild the economy. But he declared that the federal government would not set up any projects to provide workers with jobs.

Meanwhile, the problems in Kansas continued. Two years earlier, voters in Kansas had chosen representatives for their legislature. Supporters of slavery won the election. But many slavery supporters had traveled from Missouri into Kansas to cast illegal votes. Abolitionists said the election should not count. They asked that Kansas be admitted as a free state.

When Buchanan entered office, the problem had still not been solved. He supported Kansas's proslavery legislature. He said the government had been set up by its citizens, just as those of other territories had been.

Thousands of proslavery Missourians crossed into Kansas to vote illegally in elections.

John Brown believed it was necessary to use violence to fight slavery. He led attacks on proslavery settlers in Kansas.

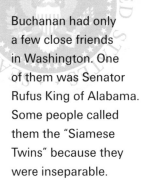

Buchanan had only a few close friends in Washington. One of them was Senator Rufus King of Alabama. Some people called them the "Siamese Twins" because they were inseparable.

Buchanan named proslavery leader Robert Walker the governor of the Kansas Territory. In October 1857, a meeting was held to create the territory's constitution. Abolitionists refused to attend. They said there were too many proslavery leaders at the meeting. So the proslavery delegates created a constitution allowing slavery. It still had to be approved by all Kansas citizens, however, and the abolitionists refused to vote on it. President Buchanan decided that the constitution was legal. He urged Congress to admit Kansas to the Union as a slave state. Congress refused to do so until all the people of Kansas decided whether to accept the constitution. In 1858, the citizens of Kansas voted on it again. They rejected the constitution by a large number of votes.

The following year, an abolitionist named John Brown and his followers attacked a building in Virginia where the government stored weapons. He planned to use the weapons to start a slave **rebellion.** Federal troops captured Brown and put him to death. The event stirred up feelings about slavery all over the nation. Some northerners felt that Brown was a good man for having fought so hard for what was right. Southerners believed he was a criminal. It was one more step on the road to war.

Buchanan did have some success as president, mostly in the area of foreign affairs. He helped create a treaty that forced the British to stop setting up colonies in the Americas. It also made the British agree to stop attacking U.S. ships in the Gulf of Mexico. When American ships were attacked off the coast of Paraguay, in South America, Buchanan sent U.S. Navy ships to fight back. Paraguay's government soon signed a treaty stating that it would no longer attack American ships.

The election of 1860 was fast approaching. By this time, Buchanan simply wanted to leave the nation's problems to someone else. He realized he had little chance of receiving the Democratic Party's nomination. Democrats from the North nominated Senator Stephen A. Douglas. Democrats from the South nominated Vice President John Breckinridge, whom Buchanan supported. This split caused problems for the Democratic Party. It helped Abraham Lincoln, the Republican candidate, win the election.

The Republican Party was founded in 1854. It was formed to oppose the expansion of slavery.

In the early days of the United States, slavery was allowed in the North as well as in the South. By the 1850s, slavery was outlawed in the North, but African Americans there still did not enjoy the same rights as white people. They could not live where they wished or get the same education as whites.

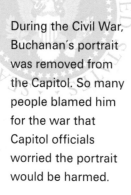

Abraham Lincoln led the United States throughout the Civil War.

Most southerners believed that Lincoln would try to end slavery. In December 1860, before Lincoln even took office, South Carolina **seceded** from the Union. In the final months of his presidency, Buchanan refused South Carolina's request to remove Union soldiers from Fort Sumter in Charleston, South Carolina. But Congress also refused to send more soldiers to defend the fort. Soon, the southerners in Buchanan's cabinet resigned. In Congress, last efforts to reach a compromise failed. The nation prepared for war and waited to see what would happen next.

By February, six more states had seceded. Buchanan bided his time until Lincoln became president. On March 4, 1861, the two men rode toward the Capitol for Lincoln's inauguration. Buchanan turned to the man who would soon be president and said, "If you are as happy, my dear sir, on entering the White House as I am in leaving it and returning home, you are the happiest man in this country!"

The Civil War began on April 12, when southern troops fired on Fort Sumter. Buchanan supported most of Lincoln's decisions during the war. But he was still the target of threats. Some people believed the war was Buchanan's fault. He finally wrote a book in his defense

During the Civil War, Buchanan's portrait was removed from the Capitol. So many people blamed him for the war that Capitol officials worried the portrait would be harmed.

ON THE EVE OF WAR

Buchanan's inability to take a stand on the slavery problem proved to be his undoing. He was never in favor of holding slaves, yet he appeared to favor the right of southerners to own slaves. Buchanan had many southerners in his cabinet. He often criticized the North. He thought the North had caused the conflict by refusing to allow the southern states to handle their own affairs.

When South Carolina seceded from the Union, Buchanan did little in response. He said states had no legal right to secede, but he also said the government could do nothing to prevent it. By doing nothing, he made it easier for other southern states to secede from the Union. As each state seceded, its congressmen and senators resigned and went back home. Soon, most of the members of Congress who remained were Republicans, and they refused to support Buchanan. His efforts to avoid war gave the southern states time to prepare for the war that would eventually come. The image to the right is a newspaper article announcing that South Carolina had left the Union.

CHARLESTON MERCURY

EXTRA:

Passed unanimously at 1.15 o'clock, P. M., December 20th, 1860.

AN ORDINANCE

To dissolve the Union between the State of South Carolina and other States united with her under the compact entitled "The Constitution of the United States of America."

We, the People of the State of South Carolina, in Convention assembled, do declare and ordain, and it is hereby declared and ordained,

That the Ordinance adopted by us in Convention, on the twenty-third day of May, in the year of our Lord one thousand seven hundred and eighty-eight, whereby the Constitution of the United States of America was ratified, and also, all Acts and parts of Acts of the General Assembly of this State, ratifying amendments of the said Constitution, are hereby repealed; and that the union now subsisting between South Carolina and other States, under the name of "The United States of America," is hereby dissolved.

THE UNION IS DISSOLVED!

Mr. Buchanan's
Administration
on the Eve of the
Rebellion was the first
presidential memoir.

*The Civil War began
on April 12, 1861.
That is when southern
troops fired on Fort
Sumter, a Union fort
in Charleston, South
Carolina. The following
day, Union forces
abandoned the fort.*

titled *Mr. Buchanan's Administration on the Eve of the Rebellion*. It was published in 1866. Unfortunately, few people read it.

James Buchanan's final years were spent at Wheatland. He entertained friends and family and read. He died quietly on June 1, 1868. On the day before his death, he told a friend, "I have no regret for any public act of my life, and history will **vindicate** my memory."

Today, Buchanan is remembered as a poor leader who could not solve the serious problems his nation faced. He had entered the presidency at one of the most trying times in American history. Unfortunately, he was not fully up to the challenge.

HARRIET LANE

Although Buchanan never married, few presidents have had a more charming and outgoing "first lady." Buchanan's niece, Harriet Lane, took charge of the duties that usually belong to a president's wife.

Harriet went to live with Buchanan at age 11, after both of her parents died. From then on, she called him "Nunc," a nickname for uncle. He called her his "mischievous romp of a niece." She easily won over British royalty and citizens when Buchanan was minister to Great Britain. When Buchanan became president, he asked Harriet to accompany him to the White House. There she acted as hostess and oversaw the housekeeping.

When Buchanan held important dinner parties for government leaders, Harriet planned the seating arrangements so that no political enemies sat next to each other. She entertained the first Japanese delegation to the United States. She hosted a dinner party, games, and a trip down the Potomac River for the Prince of Wales, who later became King Edward VII of Great Britain.

After leaving the White House, Harriet continued to care for Buchanan until 1866. Then she married a Baltimore banker, Henry Elliott Johnston. They had two sons, but both died in their teens. Her husband passed away shortly after. Harriet returned to Washington, where she worked to obtain hospital care for children and also gave money to help establish what is now the National Museum of American Art. Harriet Lane Johnston died on July 3, 1903, at the age of 73.

1790	1800	1810	1820

1791
James Buchanan is born in Cove Gap, Pennsylvania, on April 23.

1796
The Buchanan family moves to Mercersburg, where Buchanan's father builds a home and general store.

1807
At age 16, Buchanan enters Dickinson College.

1809
After graduating from college, Buchanan decides to become a lawyer. His father sends him to the town of Lancaster to work for a lawyer while he studies law.

1813
Buchanan opens a law office in Lancaster.

1814
For a few weeks, Buchanan serves as a volunteer in the War of 1812. He is elected to the Pennsylvania House of Representatives.

1816
Buchanan leaves politics and returns to his law practice.

1819
Buchanan asks Ann Coleman to marry him. After hearing false rumors that he is marrying Ann for her money, the Coleman family ends the engagement. Ann dies later that year. Buchanan is heartbroken.

1820
Buchanan is elected to the U.S. House of Representatives. He will go on to serve five terms. The Missouri Compromise is created to solve the arguments between the North and the South. It allows Missouri to enter the Union as a slave state, while Maine enters as a free state. This means that the nation maintains an equal number of slave and free states. The compromise also states that slavery is legal south of a specific latitude.

1830   **1840**   **1850**   **1860**

1831
President Andrew Jackson names Buchanan minister to Russia.

1832
Buchanan leaves for St. Petersburg, the Russian capital. He negotiates a treaty with Russia that allows U.S. ships to travel the Black Sea.

1833
Buchanan returns to the United States.

1834
Pennsylvania voters elect Buchanan to the U.S. Senate.

1845
Buchanan leaves the Senate to serve as President James Polk's secretary of state.

1846
The Mexican-American War begins.

1848
Buchanan leaves politics and purchases Wheatland, his 22-acre estate. The United States defeats Mexico and gains more than 1.2 million square miles of land.

1850
The Compromise of 1850 allows California to enter the Union as a free state, while New Mexico and Utah may decide for themselves whether to allow slavery.

1852
The book *Uncle Tom's Cabin* is published, stirring up more tension between the North and the South.

1853
President Franklin Pierce names Buchanan minister to Great Britain.

1854
While Buchanan is in Great Britain, the Kansas-Nebraska Act is passed, separating the Nebraska Territory into what will later become two states. Settlers in each place will decide whether to allow slavery. The Republican Party is formed.

1855
Fighting breaks out between pro- and antislavery forces in the Kansas Territory.

1856
Buchanan returns from Great Britain. He decides to run for president. Pro- and antislavery forces continue to battle in Kansas.

1857
Buchanan is sworn in as the 15th president of the United States on March 4. In his inaugural address, he says that the federal government should not decide whether to outlaw slavery in individual states. Two days after he enters office, the Supreme Court rules that Dred Scott, a slave, cannot sue for his freedom. It also declares that African Americans cannot be U.S. citizens and that the federal government cannot outlaw slavery in individual states.

1860
Abraham Lincoln is elected president in November. South Carolina secedes from the Union the following month.

1861
By February, six more southern states have seceded from the Union. In April, southern forces fire on Fort Sumter, a Union fort. The Civil War begins.

1865
The Civil War ends.

1866
Buchanan publishes a defense of his presidency, *Mr. Buchanan's Administration on the Eve of the Rebellion.*

1868
James Buchanan dies at Wheatland on June 1.

39

GLOSSARY

abolitionists (ab-uh-LISH-uh-nists)
Abolitionists were people who wanted to end slavery. Buchanan did not like slavery, but he was not an abolitionist.

candidates (KAN-duh-dayts)
Candidates are people running in an election. Buchanan was one of several candidates competing for the Democratic nomination for president in 1852.

civil war (SIV-il WAR) A civil war is a war between opposing groups of citizens within the same country. The American Civil War began after the southern states seceded from the Union.

compromise (KOM-pruh-myz) A compromise is a way to settle a disagreement in which both sides give up part of what they want. Congress agreed to the Missouri Compromise in 1820.

constitution (kon-stih-TOO-shun) A constitution is the set of basic principles that govern a state, country, or society. The U.S. Constitution guarantees freedom of speech and other rights for Americans.

convention (kun-VEN-shun) A convention is a meeting. Political parties hold national conventions every four years to choose their presidential candidates.

debts (DETZ) Debts are amounts of money that people owe. Buchanan did not believe that people should ask the government to pay their debts.

delegates (DEL-uh-gets) Delegates are representatives at a convention. At the 1852 Democratic convention, delegates could not agree on a candidate.

diplomats (DIP-luh-mats) Diplomats are government officials who represent their country in discussions with other nations. Buchanan served as a diplomat in Russia.

electoral votes (ee-LEKT-uh-rul VOHTS) Electoral votes are votes cast by representatives of the American public for the president and vice president. Each state chooses representatives who vote for a candidate in an election. These representatives vote according to what the majority of people in their state want.

federal (FED-er-ul) Federal means having to do with the central government of the United States, rather than a state or city government. Many people believed the federal government did not have the right to outlaw slavery.

Federalists (FED-er-ul-ists) Federalists belonged to a political party that supported having a powerful federal government. Federalists believed the United States should have a central bank.

free states (FREE STAYTS) Free states are states that banned slavery in the period before the Civil War. Southerners did not want the nation to have more free states than slave states.

inauguration (ih-nawg-yuh-RAY-shun) An inauguration is the ceremony that takes place when a new president begins a term. Buchanan gave a speech at his inauguration in 1857.

latitude (LAT-ih-tood) Lines of latitude are imaginary lines that circle the earth and are used on maps and globes for measurement. Lines of latitude measure distance from the equator.

memoir (MEM-wahr) A memoir is a book about the author's own experiences. Buchanan wrote the first presidential memoir.

mentor (MEN-tor) A mentor is a person who guides others in their life or career. Buchanan served as a mentor to his nieces and nephews.

minister (MIN-uh-stur) A minister is a person who is in charge of one part of the government. The minister to Russia is in charge of U.S. relations with Russia.

nomination (nom-ih-NAY-shun) If someone receives a nomination, he or she is chosen by a political party to run for an office. Buchanan won the presidential nomination from the Democratic Party in 1856.

political parties (puh-LIT-ih-kul PAR-teez) Political parties are groups of people who share similar ideas about how to run a government. Buchanan was a member of the Democratic Party.

politics (PAWL-uh-tiks) Politics refers to the actions and practices of the government. Buchanan had an impressive career in politics.

rebellion (ri-BEL-yun) A rebellion is a fight against one's government. Abolitionist John Brown wanted to start a slave rebellion.

seceded (suh-SEED-ed) If a group seceded, it separated from a larger group. South Carolina was the first southern state that seceded from the Union.

territory (TAYR-uh-tor-ee) A territory is a piece of land or a region, especially land that belongs to a government. The Missouri Compromise was supposed to apply to new territories in the West.

union (YOON-yen) A union is the joining together of two people or groups of people, such as states. The Union is another name for the United States.

vindicate (VIN-dih-kayt) To vindicate someone means to clear him or her from dishonor or the charge of wrongdoing. Buchanan said that history would vindicate his memory.

volunteers (vol-un-TEERZ) Volunteers are people who willingly join the military. In the War of 1812, Buchanan and other volunteers were ordered to find horses for the U.S. Army.

THE UNITED STATES GOVERNMENT

The United States government is divided into three equal branches: the executive, the legislative, and the judicial. This division helps prevent abuses of power because each branch has to answer to the other two. No one branch can become too powerful.

EXECUTIVE BRANCH

PRESIDENT
VICE PRESIDENT
DEPARTMENTS

The job of the executive branch is to enforce the laws. It is headed by the president, who serves as the spokesperson for the United States around the world. The president signs bills into law and appoints important officials such as federal judges. He or she is also the commander in chief of the U.S. military. The president is assisted by the vice president, who takes over if the president dies or cannot carry out the duties of the office.

The executive branch also includes various departments, each focused on a specific topic. They include the Defense Department, the Justice Department, and the Agriculture Department. The department heads, along with other officials such as the vice president, serve as the president's closest advisers, called the cabinet.

LEGISLATIVE BRANCH

CONGRESS
Senate and
House of Representatives

The job of the legislative branch is to make the laws. It consists of Congress, which is divided into two parts: the Senate and the House of Representatives. The Senate has 100 members, and the House of Representatives has 435 members. Each state has two senators. The number of representatives a state has varies depending on the state's population.

Besides making laws, Congress also passes budgets and enacts taxes. In addition, it is responsible for declaring war, maintaining the military, and regulating trade with other countries.

JUDICIAL BRANCH

SUPREME COURT
COURTS OF APPEALS
DISTRICT COURTS

The job of the judicial branch is to interpret the laws. It consists of the nation's federal courts. Trials are held in district courts. During trials, judges must decide what laws mean and how they apply. Courts of appeals review the decisions made in district courts.

The nation's highest court is the Supreme Court. If someone disagrees with a court of appeals ruling, he or she can ask the Supreme Court to review it. The Supreme Court may refuse. The Supreme Court makes sure that decisions and laws do not violate the Constitution.

CHOOSING
THE PRESIDENT

It may seem odd, but American voters don't elect the president directly. Instead, the president is chosen using what is called the Electoral College.

Each state gets as many votes in the Electoral College as its combined total of senators and representatives in Congress. For example, Iowa has two senators and five representatives, so it gets seven electoral votes. Although the District of Columbia does not have any voting members in Congress, it gets three electoral votes. Usually, the candidate who wins the most votes in any given state receives all of that state's electoral votes.

To become president, a candidate must get more than half of the Electoral College votes. There are a total of 538 votes in the Electoral College, so a candidate needs 270 votes to win. If nobody receives 270 Electoral College votes, the House of Representatives chooses the president.

With the Electoral College system, the person who receives the most votes nationwide does not always receive the most electoral votes. This happened most recently in 2000, when Al Gore received half a million more national votes than George W. Bush. Bush became president because he had more Electoral College votes.

THE WHITE HOUSE

The White House is the official home of the president of the United States. It is located at 1600 Pennsylvania Avenue NW in Washington, D.C. In 1792, a contest was held to select the architect who would design the president's home. James Hoban won. Construction took eight years.

The first president, George Washington, never lived in the White House. The second president, John Adams, moved into the house in 1800, though the inside was not yet complete. During the War of 1812, British soldiers burned down much of the White House. It was rebuilt several years later.

The White House was changed through the years. Porches were added, and President Theodore Roosevelt added the West Wing. President William Taft changed the shape of the presidential office, making it into the famous Oval Office. While Harry Truman was president, the old house was discovered to be structurally weak. All the walls were reinforced with steel, and the rooms were rebuilt.

Today, the White House has 132 rooms (including 35 bathrooms), 28 fireplaces, and 3 elevators. It takes 570 gallons of paint to cover the outside of the six-story building. The White House provides the president with many ways to relax. It includes a putting green, a jogging track, a swimming pool, a tennis court, and beautifully landscaped gardens. The White House also has a movie theater, a billiard room, and a one-lane bowling alley.

PRESIDENTIAL PERKS

The job of president of the United States is challenging. It is probably one of the most stressful jobs in the world. Because of this, presidents are paid well, though not nearly as well as the leaders of large corporations. In 2007, the president earned $400,000 a year. Presidents also receive extra benefits that make the demanding job a little more appealing.

★ **Camp David:** In the 1940s, President Franklin D. Roosevelt chose this heavily wooded spot in the mountains of Maryland to be the presidential retreat, where presidents can relax. Even though it is a retreat, world business is conducted there. Most famously, President Jimmy Carter met with Middle Eastern leaders at Camp David in 1978. The result was a peace agreement between Israel and Egypt.

★ *Air Force One:* The president flies on a jet called *Air Force One*. It is a Boeing 747-200B that has been modified to meet the president's needs.

Air Force One is the size of a large home. It is equipped with a dining room, sleeping quarters, a conference room, and office space. It also has two kitchens that can provide food for up to 50 people.

★ **The Secret Service:** While not the most glamorous of the president's perks, the Secret Service is one of the most important. The Secret Service is a group of highly trained agents who protect the president and the president's family.

★ **The Presidential State Car:** The presidential limousine is a stretch Cadillac DTS.

It has been armored to protect the president in case of attack. Inside the plush car are a foldaway desk, an entertainment center, and a communications console.

★ **The Food:** The White House has five chefs who will make any food the president wants. The White House also has an extensive wine collection.

★ **Retirement:** A former president receives a pension, or retirement pay, of just under $180,000 a year. Former presidents also receive Secret Service protection for the rest of their lives.

FACTS

QUALIFICATIONS

To run for president, a candidate must

* be at least 35 years old
* be a citizen who was born in the United States
* have lived in the United States for 14 years

TERM OF OFFICE

A president's term of office is four years.
No president can stay in office for more than two terms.

ELECTION DATE

The presidential election takes place every four years on the first Tuesday of November.

INAUGURATION DATE

Presidents are inaugurated on January 20.

OATH OF OFFICE

I do solemnly swear I will faithfully execute the office of the President of the United States and will to the best of my ability preserve, protect, and defend the Constitution of the United States.

WRITE A LETTER TO THE PRESIDENT

One of the best things about being a U.S. citizen is that Americans get to participate in their government. They can speak out if they feel government leaders aren't doing their jobs. They can also praise leaders who are going the extra mile. Do you have something you'd like the president to do? Should the president worry more about the environment and encourage people to recycle? Should the government spend more money on our schools? You can write a letter to the president to say how you feel!

1600 Pennsylvania Avenue
Washington, D.C. 20500
You can even send an e-mail to: president@whitehouse.gov

BOOKS

Anderson, Dale. *The Causes of the Civil War.* Milwaukee: World Almanac Library, 2004.

Baker, Jean. *James Buchanan.* New York: Times Books, 2004.

Lassieur, Allison. *James Buchanan.* New York: Children's Press, 2004.

Santella, Andrew. *James Buchanan.* Minneapolis: Compass Point Books, 2004.

Shelly, Mary V., and Sandra H. Munro. *Harriet Lane, First Lady of the White House.* Lititz, PA: Sutter House, 1980.

VIDEOS

The History Channel Presents The Presidents. DVD (New York: A&E Home Video, 2005).

National Geographic's Inside the White House. DVD (Washington, DC: National Geographic Video, 2003).

INTERNET SITES

Visit our Web page for lots of links about James Buchanan and other U.S. presidents:

http://www.childsworld.com/links

Note to Parents, Teachers, and Librarians: We routinely verify our Web links to make sure they are safe, active sites—so encourage your readers to check them out!

INDEX